# A Life in
# Poetry
## May Badman

First published in England 2006

 Quetzal Press
45 Prospect Road
St Albans
Herts. AL1 2AT

Book design and setting Francine Holland
Printed by Triographics Printers Ltd.

British Library Cataloguing in Publication Data
Badman, May
A Life in Poetry                                         ISBN  0-904763-14-5

Compiled and Edited by Chris Lakeman Fraser

Illustrations by Ray Badman

An appreciation of May and her poems by Mary Blake

Poems to May by John Cotton, John Mole,
Bill Mellors and Geoff Slater

I wish to express my grateful thanks to those friends
who have contributed to this book in poetry and prose –
Mary, Geoff, Bill, John Mole, John Cotton,
and Ray who gave his excellent drawings,
and especially Chris who instigated
and edited the book;
I send our best wishes to all who read it.

# A Life in Poetry

I was born in Greenwich, London on 10<sup>th</sup> November 1912. One of my first memories was of me being on the floor, amongst the chair legs, seeing a sunbeam. I had no words to put it in at the time, being about 18 months old. I saw this thing come down and it was pretty. It appealed to me. I wanted it. I remember reaching out for it and of course there was nothing there. I could feel it *on* my hand but not *in* my hand. I did that a couple of times and then I realized this hand was mine. I could make it do something. If I wanted to pick something up, it would do it and bring something to me. It was amazing the feeling I got. Gradually I got used to things that don't have actual bodies, like this peculiar light that you couldn't get hold of. I think I was always a bit curious about everything.

### SUNBEAM

I am that child
sitting on the floor
clutching at a sunbeam
suddenly understanding
that this was my arm
my hand
my fingers

that I could touch, take hold, bring to me
things

and reaching again
learned

that I could not hold a sunbeam,
make it mine.

When I was three, Father wanted us to be near his mother when he went off to war, so we moved to Peckham. In parts it was very countrified. It had some glorious parks and a lovely cemetery with a lot of plants where my grandmother was eventually buried. When she was alive, we hardly ever saw her because my mother was an extremely shy woman. She didn't know how to live with old people at all. She'd go to her own family. She took us down to the seaside at Worthing where her father lived with some of the family. She was one of 13 children. We used to go down to the sea. Now if you can imagine what it meant to me to be in a place where there were lovely beaches with sand and pebbles. There was grass down both sides of the street. Grandfather's family were running a big business selling fitments to the owners of grand houses. His customers came to him in fine carriages and horses.

My father thought the war would only last about 3 months but of course the training took that. He was an electrician in the Royal Engineers. We went to visit him while he was training before he went abroad. Somebody was carrying me on his shoulders. I can remember being so small, almost three. I could see tents all over the ground. I remember they took me into this one tent and the heat inside was colossal. Anyway there were about 10 or so soldiers in this tent, all of them with their sleeping mattress on the floor. Relations were visiting them all. I was being passed from one soldier to another and in the end I didn't know which one was my father.

It was about 5 years before he came back from the war. I used to ask him; 'Did you ever kill a German?' He told me once about a time when he and some of the other soldiers had got abandoned after some fighting and they were wandering, out of touch with the brigade, in *no man's land* when they came across this chateau. It was totally empty of people but there was wine in the cellar so they enjoyed that. I don't know if they had something to eat on their backs; they probably did. Then they went to bed in these silk sheets and nice soft blankets. They had a good night's rest. I wrote up the story which was printed in one of the national newspapers under the title, *Soldiers in silk sheets*.

After the war, there were no jobs, nothing was happening, no money coming in. We were very poor, a small family in a very small flat, with me as the first child. Then other children began to be born – there were five of us in the end. There was my brother who took over my pram. I didn't think a lot of him because he cried a lot. Well obviously, it's difficult for the first child. The mother has got to give special attention to the new one. Anyway, we grew up and I was looking after him to help my mother because she had got another one on the way. I grew to be very fond of him. He wasn't quite as strong willed as I was but he was a lovely man when he grew up, very gentle, very kind. And then there were my three sisters who were all spoilt but turned out lovely in the end.

My parents didn't bother with me. I wasn't happy. I was a nuisance if I didn't help. I used to grumble sometimes when I was helping her. 'Why can't Bob do something?' I didn't like the way she behaved although I loved her later in life. She was very gentle by nature but my father; he'd been spoilt by the war – the unfairness of everything. He had no principles at all it seemed to me. The only thing I did share with him was this writing business because he would copy it out sometimes so I could get it into papers. He was also interested in the theatre and used to help out at the local Empire. On one occasion he devised a play for my brother and me to perform at home.

# GREASEPAINT

Down the road was the Empire.
He'd done the electrics there, painted some of the scenery.
He had his own make-up box,
Made up sometimes to be ready for a stand-in.

At home, was his wife.
She hated the stage.
False, she said, all lies,
Fearing the cooked-up emotions
Erupting on stage.
At home too were the round faces
Of two dwarfs, two manikins
He could play with.

He pushed the chairs about,
Inventing a rushing, rocky stream,
Stood the girl on the bank of it
Cradling a doll in her arms.
The make-up round her mouth was bitter.
The skirt got in the way of her feet.

He put the boy on a chair
On the opposite bank.

He told the girl to weep and cry
How she had to drown herself and her child

And he told the boy to cry out
"Wait, I will save you"
And to jump into the river.

The child hesitated,
His moustache slipping
But at the roar of command repeated
He jumped into the swirling water,
Fell on the boulders, and weeping

Stumbled across the room to his mother,
Buried his face in her skirts.
The girl thought about the plot.
She blamed the baby.

The other thing I shared with my father was that when my brother and I were old enough to walk, and we couldn't afford buses or anything, he used to take us regularly for walks through London to all the important places and show us the big meat and fish markets. He pointed out the quarter where the Chinese lived, how they dressed and why they'd come there. He was instructing us all the time. My brother just ignored the whole lot and afterwards had to be carried home on my father's shoulders.

My parents thought I was a bit strange, I think. My mother didn't approve of my writing. In spite of this, at about 6 or 7, I started writing poems about the things about me on the table: about the sugar getting jealous of the biscuits and having an argument. I showed my mother and she said 'Oh don't worry me – its rubbish.' My Aunt said, 'Oh, my goodness, you can't have a tin of milk on the table.' She absolutely was disgusted. 'Where was the jug?' Well that became part of a poem. Another of my memories from those days involved a train late at night.

## TRAIN WHISTLE

Remember the room, north facing, cold, and laced
with fog which outside rotted the bricks,
the gutters, the very air.
Remember the iron bed, its cotton quilt
stiff as a tomb-stone, still
hoarding what light there was
in its miserly white.

Remember the whistle, teasing a child's ears
Going on and on and on. What is it?
An engine somewhere, nothing. Go to sleep.
Why does it whistle all the time? Don't ask me.
It is stuck in the fog, or broken down.
It doesn't concern you. Go to sleep.

Cold covers, hard pillow, and in the creeping dark
the far-off whistle of an engine in distress.
Perhaps it can't see the way, perhaps
the lines have gone, perhaps the driver
has got his finger stuck, perhaps
the engine has fallen over and can't get up.
Why don't they go and help it?

The house bricks melt, and all the miles between
the darkling bed and the bleating engine
are a tangled mess of torn and twisted metal.
                        The bed
lurches to iron feet, moves out and over the waste.
I'm coming, shrills the child, Wait – I'm coming!

I felt the train was in trouble and needed help. It was foggy and cold
outside. I remember saying to my mother, 'Why doesn't somebody help
it.' Nothing to do with you,' she said, 'you go to sleep.  Later I think I
must have dreamt that the bed rose up with me in it. I remember looking
down at the tops of buildings on the way to the train. This poem later won

1<sup>st</sup> Prize in a competition where the award ceremony was held on the Cutty Sark, an ancient ship in dry dock at Greenwich, with winners being given money prizes and their own wine glasses.

When I got the 11 Plus scholarship I went to Brockley Central School. I had a grant for my uniform but mum had to have that. There was no choice. But I was very lucky with the English teacher, Miss Ingram, because she praised everything I did. She had a friend who was the Geography mistress and the two of them encouraged me a lot. We had a school magazine and a poem was printed there. Miss Ingram said, "She will never go far wrong if she can write something like that at her age."

## THE AWAKENING

When a golden flood of sunlight
Pours downwards through the trees,
And a myriad leaflets tremble
At the passing of a breeze;
When the blithe birds sing their gladness
At the sun's triumphant birth,
And Heaven sheds its radiance on earth;

When the sun sets, like a ruby,
Low pendant in the west,
With fiery, red cloud-banners,
That slowly drift to rest;
When the moon casts silver shadows,
And the restless breath of Night
Doth move the ponds to sparkle in the light;

Then e'en the slowest pulse that beats
Responds to Nature's call
In every heart she stirs a chord
Which lies within us all:
A dormant sense of Beauty,
Which marketh Man from Beast.
Doth flood our hearts as sunrise floods the East.

When I was allowed to have a ticket for the public library, I didn't get out any story books. It was astronomy, science, even philosophy at times. That was, if the librarian would allow me. I think one day, I was refused altogether because I'd got knitted gloves on and the fingers were all worn out. They said I wasn't in a fit state to take a book out and I was really disappointed. Astronomy appealed to me because I wanted to know what things were all about. A lot of people in those days believed that the earth was flat. I accepted that it was round. I knew that the sun was also a round object with a constant fire going. What it burned I couldn't work out. It was one of a multitude of stars in our galaxy. I just wanted to know more all the time.

# THERE IS ONE

Of all the numberless, infinitely varying galaxies
In this reality, unbounded
Either by time or by extent,
Which we call "universe",
There is one,

And in that one, of all the million stars
That stream magnificently around its disc
There is one,

And of all the dozen attendant spheres
Drawn by it to attend its path
And limit their own,
There is one,

And on that one, amidst its thousand cities
There is one,

And in that city, of its hundred streets
There's one,

And on that street, of all the dwellings
There is one

Which has a key
Possessed by me

Within that place, my body feasts and rests,
My soul rejoices, soars and falls,

And to that one small me-place come
Moons and stars and suns,
Skies and rainbows, dreams and truth;

And to contain the stars and truth
Which throng infinity,
Of human skulls
It needs but one.

Whilst at school, I also went to night class to study arithmetic and literature but the teachers found me out and stopped me from going. When I went back to school in the Autumn term, aged 15, I should have stayed on another three months but I had to leave which I was bitterly, bitterly disappointed about. I'd got this gym slip on which I'd spent the whole of the summer holidays making. I was so pleased with it because I never had any of the uniform otherwise, except a little cap. We had arranged that I was to live with my Aunt to finish school as my parents were moving out of London. When I got to school the teacher said, "Miss Odam wants to see you. You'd better go along before we start." The headmistress said, "I think your duty is to leave school to help your parents." And I thought, 'If it's my duty, I've got to.' She said, "I've made an appointment for you and you're to go along tomorrow to be interviewed." I almost collapsed but I couldn't say very much.

It was driven into me from birth that it was important to be self supportive. I felt it was my duty to remain solvent. I didn't ever expect to earn much money from poetry.

## Urban Childhood

As a child I ran in a country of bricks,
through a land of high buildings. Tall
trams curved and tottered over
cobbled hills, the sun ran
from rooftop to rooftop flicking
chimney shadows.

It all seemed hostile. People
stared, and pushed. My turn
never came, my question, hardly asked,
was ignored. Even the nosy dogs
seemed to be saying "Shall we
bite you, little girl, who
doesn't belong
in these streets?"

and the great dray horses chose their moments
to clash and spark their giant hooves
when I was alongside, or shocked me
with their sudden steaming water
flooding the gutter. Fear pinned me
in the narrow streets, between
sweating horse-flanks, whipping draymen,
ironclad wheels, and walls of stone.

Yet there were afternoons when the sun stood still
and the pavements were empty.
A solitary sparrow pecking
on flattened dung. A butterfly sunning
on a clipped privet.
I would wander then, in the tree-lined streets,
invisible in my paradise of loneliness,
no evidence of my soul,
just my shadow,
and a silent eddy of dust.

When I started work, I moved back with my parents just outside Barking. There was an evening school going there so I used to go to evening classes. I remember an occasion when I was rushing because I was a bit late. I hurried up to the teacher with a pile of paper which I thought was all my arithmetic homework. "Eh," he said, "I don't want all this rubbish." It was my poems. There was a lot of blushing and I managed to give him the right pile.

I worked as a filing clerk in London but I was only there three months and then they sacked me. I always felt it was because of my clothes. I didn't feel I could do anything wrong in filing. It was only A, B, C after all. But they had to give me a month's notice. So I thought I'd get myself another job with more money. I searched around all the newspapers and succeeded in getting somewhere with more money.  It was a Jewish firm, which made all sorts of women's underwear.

I was writing poems like anything and I'd got pockets full of little notebooks with all these poems in.  I used to write on the tube going into work.  And these Jewish people, they were very interested in poetry, so they all wanted to see them. One or two of the books, I never got back. This second job was situated not far from the big beer-making factory and there were these huge carts and massive horses that would take all the beer around.  And of course the horses do their 'waterfalls'.  The pavements in those days were about two feet wide, not like nowadays.

After a time, I got used to the city and came to know it inside out. I left home with my middle sister – she was in a similar place to me – she didn't feel she was wanted.  So she and I took a flat in South East London.  We both worked in the city. But then I rather let her down by jumping at a chance to move to Hemel Hempstead. The office I was working in moved there at the start of war and took the staff who wanted to come.  We were found lodgings in the present high street – it was entirely different then. There was a little railway line over the road at Hemel and the lodgings were located just below the railway arch.  On the land behind, they'd got a horse.  There was a tiny teashop on the ground floor with a bedroom above it, I shared with another clerk. It was a real old cottage sort of thing with wood panels all round the walls. The rats were in there, banging around every night. And then, underneath, the old horse had itchy feet and stamped around all night trying to get rid of the itch.

Later, I found a cottage advertised in Redbourn. There was no electricity, the water came from a pump but there was a bathroom. My sister arranged to have all my furniture sent out to the cottage. It was a lovely place - real country and country people.

When that awful bombing started during the war, we had to take in all the refugees. Everybody in the village was putting up London people who had lost their homes. What you got for it was no money but a free mattress full of hay so you could sleep somebody on the floor. They were very uncomfortable things. I had about 5 different families there at one time or another. They were rough and ready Londoners who didn't understand the country. Two babies were born there in my cottage. We slept five in a bed. One night a leg of the bed went through the floorboard as I got into it. Luckily, I was prepared. We all got out, lifted it up and I covered the hole with a tin tray. We then climbed back into bed and slept well, as did the Alsatian dog which had watched the proceedings with interest.

## In Sleep

In my sleep, the smell of babies,

Half waking, fling over
Snuggle down, balled up,
Hand under pillow.

Push back damp hair
From the child's dreaming forehead.

Hold them close, the two.
Sinking, sinking
Soft, warm, dark, into their smell

There I am, I've got this daughter, a few months old, a lovely child and a son who goes to school. There came a knock on the door. It was the local policeman.

"How would you like a job in the village?"

"I'd love one," I replied, "I have been trying to earn money with my little sewing machine."

"There's this job in the village in the school meals' kitchens," he continued.

"Oh, I can't because of the baby," I said.

"You're all right there," he answered, "because there's a nursery opening in a few days time. You'll be able to put the baby in there and you'll be able to work at the school meals service as a clerk and the boy will be all right going to school." And of course I did it. I was back at work.

It was a lovely job because there was so much to do and I always like a lot to do. We did 2000 meals a day. I made up a great big blackboard with every school written down and as they rang up with the number of dinners they wanted I put it on the board. I had to look after five vans and drivers and make sure our own petrol pump was filled up. I had to fill in forms for the council to say what nourishment there was in the food; watch the cost as well. I worked there for 17 years.

Revd. D. Bickerton, vicar at St Mary's Church, Redbourn

One evening, I went along to the church and waited for the vicar to come out.
"Would you baptise my two children?" I said.
"Yes of course I would and what about you?"
"Isn't it too late?" I said,
"No it isn't," he said, "God is there, he's waiting." He was so good at explaining it all that I didn't feel I was committing myself to something that wasn't true.
And I thought, 'Well there must be something there.'

So that moment when I met the vicar outside the church door, changed my life completely. He treated me as someone to be respected and he took an interest in the poetry. This is what really brought me into contact with the poetry world. He wrote a bit himself but he put all his energy into being a vicar. He was a lovely man. He told me about T.S.Eliot, Gerard Manley Hopkins and Ezra Pound. It was fascinating. And when he found out I was writing he gave me a regular time early on Wednesday evenings. He would read what I had written and was a good critic. He really tore them to pieces in some places. I could understand what he was trying to do with me. I got to love the language for itself through him. It really was very good. It went on for about four years. He also set me to work as the Parish Secretary. I used to arrange outings for the villagers.

Both the children were in the choir and I also put them in the Scouts and the Girl Guides. My daughter did well at school. The teachers used to make her a prefect all the time because she would look after the other children – but she never passed any exams. When she was 15, she came up to me and said, "I'm leaving school, I've got a job". She told me she was going to do it, and she did it. It was in Hemel Hempstead with British Rail – and they were just bringing out computers and she dropped straight into it. They were taking on people, training them to use computers. That was their job and she's been in computers ever since.

### THE LAMP (A BIRTHDAY GIFT)

Light of my life, she said,
Giving me the lamp.
Lovely words
From a daughter.

Her smile was doubtful,
Almost rueful.
I wasn't sure, she said,
If you would want it.

The memory lit. In the fifties
Our cottage, tumbling about our ears,
Was lit with lamps
And smelt like a church.

Oil, and soot,
Wick-trimming,
The dribbling can
In the bottom of the baby's pram.

Sun on straw,
Ice in the bath,
Hens underfoot,
Doorsteps lost under snow.

The roaring range,
Live nestling on the hearth,
Bats, moths, cuckoos, moles,
Snow-drops, Victorias, Kentish cobs.

The year's disciplines,
The year's gifts,
The church in the village,
A stone hump under the common,
The changing vestments, frontals,
Flowers, corn, holly,
Christmas roses. Christ,
Were ever times so sweet?

Home, in the dark.
The scratch-flare of a match,
A bud of orange on the wick,
Its lock of smoke.

By the muttering light, then,
We saw one another.

*There, turn it down,*
*Let the glass grow warm.*

*Now, I say*
*Let's light it. See if I can*
*Remember.*

After the war, all the School Meal Kitchens were closed one by one and I was moved to Chiswell Green, before that too was closed. Then there was nothing; no immediate job or source of money. I drew out my pension money from the Council and bought a knitting machine. The work was interesting but the villagers gave me the most difficult jobs, e.g. garments with button holes, and the money came in too slowly.

However, down the road towards Hemel Hempstead there was a firework factory. It was at the time when countries in our Empire were becoming independent and they all wanted fancy fireworks. So I went down there and said, "I'd like a job. Have you got one?" Yes, they had, so I started. Gosh that was an experience. They were all so nervously strung because they were experimenting all the time. It was a farm with lots of little huts which were covered with stuff that stopped the sun getting in and setting all the gunpowder off. Every so often there would be a bang, as though it was the war again. One of the managers had only got one thumb. Partly my job was filling in endless forms for exporting the stuff and finding ships which had the proper safety facilities.

It was a lovely two years but I didn't think I could stick it much longer. That was when my boss said to me, "Have you done these forms yet?" "Nearly done," I said, "but I want some pins."

Verulam Writers' Circle, St Albans Town Hall. *Evening Echo, Hemel Hempstead, 1974*

"Ah." He chucked a big drawer of pins all over me; in my clothes and hair and everything.

"Oh," I said, "I don't know, I don't fancy this much."

So I worked the week out and went to work for the old peoples' home in St Albans.

The last full-job I had was in the BMA, dealing with Indian doctors. I had to look up the various hospitals they had been in and check their standards. It was well paid and well thought of but I lost it because of illness.

At 19 my daughter got married. I couldn't be in the house when she left. I grieved. It went on about three months. I used to wander round the village and sometimes one of them would call me, because they all knew me,

"Come and have supper with us."

But I wouldn't go into my house until it was dark and time for bed. Then I'd get up and go to work alright.

But then suddenly I thought, "You are an idiot; you've got all this time and all that poetry waiting."

I looked in the paper and found an advert for the Verulam Writers' Circle. I was very inclined to be nervous of new situations. I'd never been to a writing class like that. I remember I got on my bicycle, it was a summer's evening; had a job to find this place – not too far from St Peter's church. I don't know if I read anything the first time – probably not. It seemed overwhelming, all these wonderful people who really wrote books; knew how to do it. It was lovely.

# Verulam Writers' Circle

## Spontaneous Writing competition (10 minutes)

SHAKESPEARE

WATCHING SHAKESPEARE

ON TELEVISION

'Forsooth, what's this, can these glass figures be
Mine own?  'Tis nought but blasphemy!
What tongue is this – and what's that harp, that drum –
Not in my directive, by my thumb!
And look – that boy's a female, ne'er a man –
This cuts me so, look I no longer can.
I'll turn the switch, and see what other play
Is being wafted through the air – it may
Be lesser, but the less distorted, torn.
Ah – what is this? – a maiden, all forlorn
Because of dandruff? - I can stand no more,
Shall haunt this place no more, shall ne'er return,
Yet will the memory burn, but ever burn."

Thus spake the shade, of shades that spake and play'd
The master's works, the master's words, that fade
Never upon the page, nor on the stage –
Yet on the screen they run like candle-wax,
and lose their shape, and tangle myth and fax.

Mixing with the writers in the Circle, I started to think about publication. I wanted it so much. I got to hear about Howard Sergeant who was a poet but who also edited other poets' work. I wrote to him, he liked my work and eventually published it in 1964 under the title, *Night is another World*. The joy of having it was wonderful.

### NIGHT

Night is another world.
Dusk deepening, descending,
Drawing away
The clamorous colours of the day,
Leaving but light and shade.

Mushrooms gleam, there are lamps
In the damp grass, and the winding path
Is lit with sad white flowers
Floating dimly in the hedge.

Mist floats the tree-tops
As in a silent sea,
And here discloses
A world below a world.

Deeper the dusk descends
Till the dark ocean of night
Softens shape into shadow,
The last of the light
Has gone.

A sour moon thrusts through ragged cloud,
And stars begin to cry aloud;
The glow- worm in the long wet grass
Lights nothing but himself.

Let us go in to the dry lights
And day-time sanity caught between four walls,
For there the air is ordinary and warm,
And night asks nothing of us
But to draw the shade.

VER POETS began life in 1966. It was then known as the St Albans & District Poetry Club and came about at the suggestion of St Albans Arts Council when they approached the Verulam Writers' Circle. At that time the Writers' Circle was chaired by Joan Rice; I was their secretary and also a member of the Arts Council. Joan and I decided to call a public meeting to found the poetry club. As I was a member of the executive council of the London-based Poetry Society we were able to invite the Society's programme organiser, Joan Murray Simpson, to come and speak. She was an attractive and eloquent speaker and we finished with the names of thirty interested people.

We formed a small cornmittee and received a grant from St Albans Arts Council of £3 (not quite a useless amount in those days!). We were an active group, all writing, and poetry was at an exciting stage then, very heady times. Finding a permanent home for the club proved to be a serious problem. We were offered a photographic studio meeting amongst tripods, cameras and back-screens; we tried various public houses, but did not drink enough to please our hosts; then a room in a community centre, sandwiched between a dancing class and a hands-on first aid demonstration. Our numbers fell drastically and it seemed hopeless to try and go on.

However, I thought we could make a fresh start. After some discussion with Ray, my husband, by that time chairman (we were a committee of two — poets generally I found were not very practical and Joan Rice had withdrawn to concentrate on her duties with the Verulam Writers' Circle) I decided on a name, the Ver Poets, and offered membership to people outside the district.   Thus we developed with a local and postal membership, which covers all of the UK and with members living abroad.

At the same time, we were offered a room in an old house used by the International Centre. This was absolutely central, just behind St Albans City Hall in Bricket Road, and car parking was simple but no chairs or tables were available. The centre itself, doing splendid work for incoming people from many different nations, was nevertheless operating on a shoe-string. We used the local press to appeal for old furniture which might be lying unused and forgotten in attics and sheds, and during the next couple of weeks gathered an assortment of chairs and couches, coffee tables, even a carpet of sorts, and soon fitted up our room with a kettle and mugs.

We met there for the next ten years. Then it seemed a pity only to use our room only on alternate Monday evenings and we ran a poetry parlour every Saturday from 9 to 4 where poets could call in at any time to read their poems, talk and have coffee. Jeff Cloves (of Snorbens Diary fame in the St Albans Review) was a regular visitor, with his guitar, and several other members sang or played. We formed a performing group of poets and musicians with John Mole, Roger Burford-Mason and others, travelling as far afield as Nottingham, Berkhamstead and the Poetry Society in London.

Another project was a stall in St Albans market every Saturday, to sell the poetry pamphlets we were by that time producing, duplicating pages with jelly-roller and decorating card covers by hand. Concrete poetry was the rage and we had a lot of fun with that, both orally and in print. The stall was not popular with other stall-holders at first. We did not follow the market conventions and often some of our more youthful members would gather beneath the stall writing poems and practising their guitars. However, we did eventually make friends, and when rain filled the top of our canvass awning they rallied round to help. We did sell some poetry and sometimes covered the cost of the stall; but after about three months, with winter coming on, we abandoned the project.

Further changes were to come. The house we were using was condemned on account of dry rot and closed. Fortunately, one of our members, John Mole, was teaching English at St Albans School and arranged for us to rent the English room there. This was full of the right literary atmosphere, lined with books of poetry and I was delighted. Some of the members missed the freedom of Bricket Road, but it was more practical, secure and quiet at the school and we could really write and study there. Thanks to John Mole, we later moved into the larger English Studio, a lovely light room.

# ┌─Serenade for a 'Queen'─┐

**POETRY AND FOLK SINGING GROUP ENTERTAIN THEIR FAVOURITE GUEST**

The Queen Mum of St Albans, Mrs Sylvia Battcock, relaxed contentedly last night as she listened to members of Ver Poets sing folk songs and read poetry... Mrs Battcock, who has taught public speaking at St Albans College for the past 18 years, is a great favourite amongst the young people of St Albans who gave her the nickname.

*Evening Echo, Hemel Hempstead, 14th July 1970*

As the group increased in size, Roger Burford-Mason became our first President with Howard Sergeant as Vice President. We were distraught when Roger emigrated to Canada. John Cotton was then invited to be President with John Mole as Vice President and the two of them arranged our music and readings all over the country. On John Cotton's death, John Mole accepted the presidency with Carole Satyamurti agreeing to be Vice President. Carole was a well known poet and long-time member of Ver Poets and adjudicator of VER POETS OPEN COMPETITION. We are greatly indebted to all who have so acted for their tremendous and ongoing support. And finally, it must not go without saying that my husband and our chairman over so many troubled and untroubled years, Ray Badman, has been a brick throughout.

We now have many established poets as members, as well as beginning writers and those who want to recover the good habits of their youth before the world took over! I feel that poetry is a major part of British, and Western, culture, involving thought and language and the bringing to bear of objective skill on to the deepest of our emotions. I am very wary of the tendency towards the abuse of sex and violence in the arts, and the loss of respect and esteem generally. But there are great writers today whose work will last, because they are sincere and have not bent the knee to fashion.

Ver Poets' present activities include regular programmes with visiting poets, workshops and competitions. The annual Open Competition is well supported.

I met Ray when he joined Ver Poets.  We married in 1968 and he became Chairman soon after.

May and Ray at St Michael's Church Hall on the evening of the celebration of the Verulam Writers' Circle's 50th Anniversary Celebrations.

Photo courtesy of K.J.Bennett.

# Husband

When the mower stops, for no apparent reason,
Though I shake it, switch it off and on,
Unplug, replug, with no result, no churning of the grass,
I want to howl for him like a child with a broken toy.
Sure enough, he hears that the motor's stopped
And comes like a father and says, "I'll see to it",
And I feel comforted. Then when he's scything or raking,
Or shifting something in a wheelbarrow,
I want to tag along after him, not doing anything,
Not busy, but idly watching his strength, his slow persistence,
I want to interrupt him, be a nuisance,
Say "would you move this, from there to here,
It is so difficult for me. Would you do it now,
If you don't, you'll forget, and it won't be done."
In the end he does it, not impatient,
As he would throw a stick for a persistent puppy
Or let in the miawing cat, and says to me "There,
It's not the end of the world."
And I am comforted,
Let him go on with his heaving,
Or his tending of the rubbish,

It's regal smoke bonfire, a column
Of blue vapour at the top
A petal of flame flowering at the base,
As he stands with the fork
Authority, needing no exertion, the fire
Tame, obedient.
And I am comforted, and move away
With that picture of him in my head
In his garden clothes, his unconsciousness
Of the seething field, the beauty of the milkwort,
The spangling sun opening golden flowers,

And now I recognise that it is enough
That these things exist for me
He's part of them, knife and hook and rake,

Grass amongst grass, consumed, consuming,
Smoke, flame and light
And I must make supper soon,
Say things to him he does not hear,
And be content

## AFTER YOU'D GONE

The world became a different place
When you had gone. We had plodded
Single file along the path, you setting the pace
In your decent suit and your bag of nightwear and books,
I behind in house-shoes, ducking
Tall spires of nettles,
Neither of us caring or giving thought
To the chaos, the calamity we caused
By our hurried passage through this early silence,
This gentle mist, this full, this crowded emptiness.

After we broke from the path to where
Gardens lapped grass and gravel against the houses
With roses and begonias afire in the haze,
Where the field lay like a sea to the distant landfall
Of far-off woods, and we stepped out the last few yards
To the turn, I let you go. Standing
I watched time remove you, shrink your shape
Till with a last wave you were consumed
By those private bushes into another road.

I stood, while the world composed itself,
Erased our footsteps and our voices,
Settled the silence and relaid the mist.
Houses, empty of consciousness
Held blank stares of glass, unmoving curtains,
Expensive ornament and order.
They seemed unreal. I turned and stood by the field.

Far off, small in the haze were horses, grazing.
What made them see me, what made them come,
One by one to lift their heads and gaze
While the thought came and the intention jelled,
The action began?

Slowly they came, so that I saw the curves of their flanks
Framing their long nodding heads,
Growing, enlarging, with every deliberate unhurried step.
They came close to the wire, mouths drooling grass,
I stroked their cheeks, their ears,
They agreed I should.
Those large sombre eyes needed to use no words,
They wanted nothing of me, they were giving, not asking.
They turned sideways and stayed, cropping
And I listened to the crisp sounds,
Running my hands over the broad solid warmth
Of their hide, the bay and the brown.

I began slowly to walk towards home,

They walked with me, not denying
The comfort of their presence as long as I needed it,
The firm warmth of them somehow reminded me of my mother,
Of her warm apron, and the bread she made,
Before all that fell apart.

I don't ever sit down deliberately to write poetry except in class when I
have to. But at home I might be doing anything and an idea will come or
some incident will occur and I've just got to grab a pen.

## Finding the Curve

The poem hit me, and it sprang
Into the curve as a rainbow does
When sunbeams leap through the drenched air.

It has no reality yet, its life
No cogency, its purpose
Hidden in that place where rainbows are
Before they come. I am to hold it
Keep it in balance, tense, as a bow
Holds the arrow before it flies.

So it is a matter of fingers, and the pen,
And my heart which have the knowledge
That I, earthbound, must find and trust
Then let the arrow go,
Watch the rainbow curve as it becomes
A leaping horse, or the seagulls I saw,
Flying stars on a black sky.

I always felt close to nature. When I was little the house was always
running with mice. I was thrilled with them. They ran up the curtains.

They were my playmates and companions. The cat I used to dress up in baby clothes. They felt close to us as humans.

I remember much later as an adult, standing on a bridge over a river, watching swans flying overhead. They were squawking as though they were pleased with themselves. I felt as if I could go with them to some exciting place.

## Swans flying

They could not be caught, those flying birds.
Painted, their movement would be lost.
Remember, for a second they fly again,
Their long white wings like paddles in the sea.
They moved as music, three strong notes in white,
Kept, self imposed within the stave,
And a forth, grey brown, the cygnet,
Centred in the family.
Ambitious youth, now high, now low, but only
By little, soon to achieve
That instinct perfection. The breeze
Brushed sweet and clean and cold against our faces
Where we leant against the rail above the river,
Broad here, breast stippled blue,
Sweeping a giant curve through emerald turf.

The harmony curled to diminuendo
As the birds, far away, turned on some course
We could not know. We left the bridge
Gold echoed in the sky; a flicker of white
Far off, tipped a tree and touched a cloud,
A final, fading chord.

There is something in us – not just flesh and blood – religion comes into it to some extent. There must be an answer to why we're here. There has to be a purpose. I feel I want to get closer to find out what it's all about.

## Resolution

I shall not call you winter
You who have veined my hands
But stubbornly stay in autumn
Build castles with those sands

They say are running out;
And I shall tip the glass,
Make what was empty, full,
Take all that comes to pass.

For time is only time
Leaked from eternity.
Where Abraham was, He is
Who taught us sanctity:

So though the years have marked
And scarred my slackening
                              skin,
I will say I am a soul
Weathered, and well run in.

## Self-Assessment

I stand like a tree,
my leaves are my thoughts.
I look through my bark
to the rings of my time
to see what I was, what I am; my leaves
flutter in the breeze.

I see myself as a self selfish –
wanting, forever wanting –
a sunbeam, a rainbow, – all the sun
things – a ball, a hoop, a rope, a top to spin,
books, books, books – my first library ticket
was gold.

I wanted flowers, trees, the fields, woods, mountains –
the Earth,                            I wanted it all.
People.        –       I wanted people
Love, I wanted to love, to be loved,

I see myself a self selfish,
A conifer, or British apple

I don't change –
I have almost all I want.

Grateful?

Yes!

# A WRITER'S LIFE

At first there were things, many things
Available for her practical study.
Doors became interesting – when their latches were not too high.
Stairs she climbed, but could not descend.

School, when it came, gave her letters, words, books
And soon, writing.
Her early work took the form of verse
And pouring life into inanimate objects
Had the milk converse with the sugar
The butter-dish quarrel with the jam.
She showed a poem to her mother
"Rubbish" was that busy lady's comment,
"Take it away – do something useful!"
When she tried for a kinder critique from her aunt,
That well-mannered relative was shocked, she exploded
"You can't have a TIN on the dining table!"

School took her on through Wordsworth, Byron and Shelley,
And encouraged by Miss Ingram (English),
She contributed to, and edited, the School Magazine, her style
Changing accordingly,
But the new Head was to strike a blow
"Your duty", said that stern, if earnest personage,
"is to help your parents. You must leave school and take a post
"I have arranged an interview....."

Thus her pockets bursting with note-books,
She began work as a junior clerk in the Big City
Finding it hard to believe that so much money would come to her
At the end of the month,
For so little work.
In the tube going home that first day
She mourned – I have not learned
anything
today.

The years rolled on, she lived a full life.
Her work appeared in many magazines, UK and USA
Some pamphlet books appeared, and 3 awards for her
services to poetry.
In her advancing age she is still writing,
Ambitious, and looking for a publisher.

# Friends and fellow poets

## May by Mary Blake

I first met May in 1992, a friend took me to have tea with her in her cottage outside St Albans, in fact entering her cottage is to enter another time. I showed May what I used to call my word pictures, poetry I thought was something others did. May said, "You are writing poetry, come and join us at VER." Needless to say I did, and from May I learnt so much. So many poets she has encouraged owe such a debt to May and in fact she has dedicated her life to VER and to poetry. May is one of those rare beings who have always written, her poems are like small jewels. She can write about the most mundane, ordinary things like washing up, cutting hair, looking at a horse in a meadow and turns them into magic.

## REPETITIONS AND DEVIATIONS

Each day I feed the cats and birds
And grieve in passing
That I have not hoovered the house for ages
And have bought too many books and
Too many plants in pots and too many clothes,
And haven't been to church nor prayed exactly
But I do think, yes, I think and wonder
And ponder about all these wars
And starvations and people in Africa and London
With no money and nowhere to live, and
I think it is not good literature to have all those 'ands'
And no conclusion, and how can there be
When the great question behind it all remains unsolved,
Like has God seeded this one small globe with intelligent beings
Is earth the only green oasis in a universe of fire
And dead rock, and is God?
Is he? and if not is it worth while
Struggling to turn our course around

From cruelty, destruction and war?
I am not alone, except that every I is alone,
Millions of us, sparks of existence, each
Caged in our flesh, driftwood in a cataract
And only the falls ahead
Which reminds me
Today, I must wash my hair.
Near as we are to Hell, we are near to Heaven,
And I would be clean.

In her book "Strawberries in the Salad" there is a poem, "Light Fingers"
that haunts me, the last verse makes my neck tingle.

## Light Fingers

You came in daylight
At the shopping hour
Slid through the hedge
Limbed lightly up to the balcony
And found the only door we'd left unlocked.

Quick in the bedroom, you touched everything
Yet left everything untouched
Save a watch which clung to your thumb,

Downstairs you bolted our door,
Our exit and our entrance
And opened your means of escape.
From room to room you stepped
High heeled like Pan, flinging
All inner doors wide
And took a clock.

Why did you come?
So little suited you.
A fast worker,
But you took your time.
We blundered in, you flew

Safe and away
Between the silence
Along the dumb lane

And yet
You have never left.
We share our house
With you.

Another down to earth poem is "String Beans", it holds so much love for
the world.

### String Beans

They say you may leave the bean haulms in
For another year.

If I were a bean
I would care for that,

After death
And a decent interval

To come up again
In the same place,

The supporting framework
Waiting there.

How joyfully I would spring,
And be how much

Finer a plant,
Earlier

Beanier,
And, as the season wore on

Definitely less stringy.

In "Old Crocks", chipped plates become old people and ends with such joy for a dandelion.

### Old Crocks

Chipped plates,
Saucers without cups,
Cups minus handles,
Pots without lids –
These are old people,
Cracked and stained and missing parts,
Missing mates, and nowhere matching.

Yet many an old plate we will treasure,
A lidless teapot, lovely with roses;
Old saucers compliment different cups.

If I should be left
Graceless, useless,
With none of the same pattern
Any more around me,
Let me hold daisies, grass, and wet-the beds
For some child who loves to pick flowers.


May can show pathos in "The other half of the bed", again so matter of fact yet so full of deep love.

### The Other Half of the Bed

The other half of the bed is empty
Cool where warmth once radiated
From his hard long limbs.  I use it now
As a place to leave my books, and tomorrow
As I drink my morning tea I shall
Spread our letters there, his and mine.

The time between, when I pull the light
And the dark drops down and kills today,
When now is not today, and not tomorrow,
Is when my feet will stray
Searching for the warmth that is not there,
When I shall have no signal when to turn,
No heavy arm to belt me down
And sentence me to sleep. Upon my lids

He will float in his iron bed, in his bright far
ward,
Lit up there, and with a glass between us.


Her humour fills her work in "The Visitor", she turns a meeting over tea into pure magic, and she takes us into another dimension.


## The Visitor

I said to him "Why
Have you come so late?"
          He lifted his wings
Slightly, his way
Of shrugging his shoulders
          His beak
Of pure gold opened a little
And his tongue gave a cheeky
          Amethyst loll.

"Take a chair" I said, "if you'd like to.
          The cakes I made
Are still fresh, and the elixir
          Is in the refrigerator."

On ivory talons he crossed the grass
          To the chairs
And he took his perch

On the back of one,
Arranging his gorgeous tail and smoothing a feather
On his gleaming breast. I went
To fetch drinks and in each
I popped a diamond. The biscuits
Were flakes of gold, they
Had cost me the earth.
He drank, bending his head
Clattering the jewels in his crest.
I sat, passing him food
And we conversed
Until dusk. A moon
Rose from the trees. He leapt
Silently from the chair

And brushing my hand lightly
With one wing tip, he said
"I must go. It's been so nice. I'm sorry
I was late."

I watched him go. His great wings
Lifted him over the hedge
And for a moment I saw his
Glittering outline
Against the moon.

How to describe May? Perhaps just to say that she loves life, nothing escapes her from a blade of grass, a small shell, bird or man, to the remotest star, she instils all with love.

# For May
### by John Cotton

May,
Whose life has spanned wars,
Continents and children,
With the same fine tenacity
You sustained your brain-child
The Ver Poets.
With a membership that embraces
Nations and generations,
It is a Society you enhanced
With your own poems:
Always precise, proper and frequently poignant.
So we rejoice with you in a life of poetry,
And the generosity and kindness that informed
All you created and cherished,
And which benignly coloured our lives.
Now with love we celebrate your ninety years,
So full of activity and energy,
It shames us younger ones
Who imagine we are getting old!
Another ninety to come?
Well hang on in there May,
If anyone could do it, you could!

## Taking Care

(extract)
by John Mole

.........poetry in you has taken care as you
Have done for others, going inexhaustibly

about its business, day-by-day,
a gift as generous in self-effacement
as your friendship. Even as I write

I guess that you'll be writing too, a poem
or maybe notes for one. How can you help it?

# To May Ivimy – a Friend to Poets
by Bill Mellors

Alone with a dream of words.
Searching to paint the colour of an unseen sky
Sound the richness of laughter
Provoke the rustle of imagined fear
Or bring to the current minute
The past intensity of long ago half remembered love.

We have all been there,
With the urgent message waiting its call.
But the expectant pen
Droops in the uncertain hand
And the white sheet of paper
Receives only inadequate translation

But we who knew May
Have heard her quiet voice
And the words we did not know we possessed
Burst from some dungeon of the mind
And the sky and the laughter
The fear and that long ago love
Illuminate the solid blankness of the page

May, friend of poets
And the poetry within

# Gobbling the Moon
### by Geoff Slater

Sitting shaving, half an eye on a travelling clock
Contemplating everybody else's navels,
I didn't notice the hands were still....

I watched you gobbling moons;
Taming corncrakes in the fireplace,
Teaching them to make a kinder noise;

Rampaging on your bicycle
Humming plainchant
With personalised number plates.

Out of the back of my mind I saw you,
An elderly mole with pointed eyes,
A good natured eagle that's mislaid its claws,

Curling to catch, pick glimpses of us
With the fine discrimination of a thoughtful cat
Choosing snacks from neighbourhood kitchens;

Bolstered by double damasked pillows,
Scribbling us down in bed,
Fun dripping onto your spectacles.

You should eat toasted muffins at tea-time
With Cornish butter and Greek honey
From the mountain with the funny name.

.....and so I was late and said nothing,
but wrote this. It is a picture
I want to keep.
            And share.

# Poems  by May Ivimey Badman

## May Badman

May Badman is a poet whose work has appeared in many journals including *The Literary Review, Poetry Review, Time and Tide, Tribune, Workshop New Poetry, Meridian, Grand Piano, Pembroke Magazine* – Pembroke University, USA, *Hertfordshire Countryside* and *Country Life*. Among the anthologies in which her poems have been published are *New Poetry* – Arts Council Of Great Britain, *Contemporary Women Poets* – Rondo, *Without Adam* – Femina Books, *Poems of the Medical World* – MTP Press Ltd; *and anthologies for schools by* Harrap, O.U.P., Macmillan and I.L.E.A.

Her previous collections include *Late Swings* – Mandeville Press, *Midway this Path* – Manifold, *Night is another World* – Outposts, *My House* – Dodman Press. In 1981 she won first prize in the Greenwich Festival Poetry Competition.

For some years she was a member of the Executive Council of the Poetry Society and Honoury Treasurer. Also as a member of the Society of Women Writers and Journalists, she served on their Council for many years. She was on the committee of the St Albans Arts Council until it ceased in 1982. She has also organised the Michael Johnson Memorial Poetry Competition from 1972 to 1982.

She has received three awards for services to poetry including the Dorothy Tutin Prize and one where the award was an invitation to a garden party at Buckingham Palace.

Under her married name of May Badman, she founded and organised Ver Poets from 1966 to 2004 and edited its magazine Poetry Post. Ver Poets now has hundreds of local and postal members in Britain and abroad. As it grew in size, May ceased to send out her work although she continued to write and for many years has attended Master Class Poetry Courses at Madingley Hall, Cambridge University with Roger Garfitt as tutor – so close to the University which she had longed to attend. Ver Poets is now run by a committee because in 2004 May gave up running it as the result of ill health but she is Patron to the group.

Of her book *Parting of the Leaves* it was said
> 'this poet writes from the depth of her being.....
> language, structure and metric patterning
> are at one with the movement of emotion and
> understanding' (*Pembroke State University Magazine*)

## Chris Lakeman Fraser

Film editor, journalist and writer. Film credits include BAFTA award-winning *Baka –People of the Forest* and articles for the *Independent, Guardian, Financial Times, Bookseller* and *Author* magazines.

## Ray Badman

Highway technician, Normandy veteran, artist and for many years Chairman of Ver Poets.

## ROCKABYE BABY

The tree top is strong, its great arms
Hands and fingers full of leaves
Gently rocking me. The moon sways
And stars blink between boughs.

The birds sing, for dawn is coming.
Blackbirds, thrushes, wood pigeons,
A shower of tits and sparrows.
I was asleep, but now

In my creaking cradle I can hear the wind,
Its rhythmic blowing, hush and puff
Like a baby's breath. Now

I hear it stopped. Behind the birds is silence,
And they, one by one,
Fall quiet.

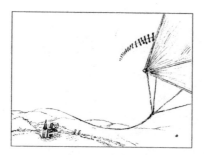